A Note to Parents

DK READERS is a compelling program for beginning readers, designed in conjunction with leading literacy experts, including Dr. Linda Gambrell, Professor of Education at Clemson University. Dr. Gambrell has served as President of the National Reading Conference and the College Reading Association, and has recently been elected to serve as President of the International Reading Association.

Beautiful illustrations and superb full-color photographs combine with engaging, easy-to-read stories to offer a fresh approach to each subject in the series. Each DK READER is guaranteed to capture a child's interest while developing his or her reading skills, general knowledge, and love of reading.

The five levels of DK READERS are aimed at different reading abilities, enabling you to choose the books that are exactly right for your child:

Pre-level 1: Learning to read
Level 1: Beginning to read
Level 2: Beginning to read alone
Level 3: Reading alone
Level 4: Proficient readers

The "normal" age at which a child begins to read can be anywhere from three to eight years old. Adult participation through the lower levels is very helpful for providing encouragement, discussing storylines, and sounding out unfamiliar words.

No matter which level you select, you can be sure that you are helping your child learn to read, then read to learn!

LONDON, NEW YORK, MUNICH,
MELBOURNE, AND DELHI

Editor Julia Roles
U.S. Editor John Searcy
Production Georgina Hayworth

Reading Consultant
Linda Gambrell, Ph.D.

Produced by
Shoreline Publishing Group LLC
Editorial Director James Buckley, Jr.
Designer Tom Carling, carlingdesign.com

First American Edition, 2007
Published in the United States by DK Publishing
345 Hudson Street, New York, New York 10014

Copyright © 2007 Dorling Kindersley Limited

Dorling Kindersley is represented in Canada by
Tourmaline Editions Inc
662 King Street West, Suite 304
Toronto, Ontario M5V 1M7

DK books are available at special discounts when purchased in bulk
for sales promotions, premiums, fund-raising, or educational use.
For details, contact: DK Publishing Special Markets, 345 Hudson
Street, New York, New York 10014, or SpecialSales@dk.com

A catalog record for this book
is available from the Library of Congress.

ISBN: 978-0-7566-3139-0 (Paperback)
ISBN: 978-0-7566-3142-0 (Hardcover)

Color reproduction by Colourscan, Singapore
Printed in U.S.A.

16 17 18 23 22 21 20 19
019 - 191971 - AUG/07

The publisher would like to thank the following for their kind
permission to reproduce their photographs:
(b = bottom; c = center; t = top)
Alberta Provincial Parks: 26, 32, 34t, 47; American Museum
of Natural History: 14; Canada Fossils: 16t; Corbis: 21b; Getty
Images: 15t, 19t; Dreamstime.com: 14t, 26t, 27t, 33t, 34b; Glenbow
Archives: 17, 19; Library Archive Canada: 12; Courtesy of Natural
Resources Canada: 7, 10t, 11t, 11b; Photos.com: 38c, 39b; Julia
Roles: 4, 6t, 8, 10b, 28; Royal Ontario Museum: 20b; Courtesy
Royal Tyrrell Museum/Alberta Tourism, Parks, Recreation and
Culture (www.tyrrellmuseum.com): 9, 13t, 16b, 20t, 22, 25t, 29
(2),33b, 44c, 45t, 45b.

All other images © Dorling Kindersley.
For more information see: www.dkimages.com

Discover more at
www.dk.com

Contents

 **READERS**

Dinosaurs!
Battle of the Bones

Written by Sharon Siamon

DK DK Publishing

Bones in the badlands

Gazing up at giant dinosaur skeletons in a museum, marveling at their great height and massive jaws, do you wonder how such creatures walked the earth for 150 million years and then vanished, leaving only fossil bones behind?

If you want to explore the world of dinosaurs, a great place to visit is the Red Deer River Valley. Also known as Dinosaur Valley, this amazing badlands valley appears suddenly out of the prairies of Alberta, Canada, like the landscape of a lost world. In places you can hardly take a step without landing on a dinosaur fossil.

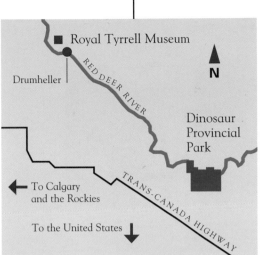

Some of the most exciting dinosaur research in the world is done here at the Royal Tyrrell Museum. Its famous paleontologists and field workers find new fossils—often new species—every year.

This book tells the story of the early discoveries in Dinosaur Valley, the scientists who study the dinosaur fossils, and some of the famous dinosaurs that have been found there.

Where is the valley?
Dinosaur Valley stretches along the Red Deer River in southeastern Alberta. It extends from Drumheller in the north to Dinosaur Provincial Park in the south.

Frightening sight

Joseph Tyrrell's hand shook as he clutched his rock hammer. "What is that?" he gasped. It was August 11, 1884. Tyrrell was twenty-six and searching for coal in the Red Deer River Valley. Suddenly, he was face-to-face with huge gaping jaws, jutting out of the cliff.

"As I stuck my head around a point," he wrote, "there was this skull leering at me, sticking right out of the rock. It gave me a fright."

Lots of coal
Joseph Tyrrell's discovery of coal in Dinosaur Valley was the foundation of a coal mining industry near Drumheller.

He had found the "large and fairly perfect head of . . . a gigantic carnivore." It had teeth as big as long spikes.

Dinosaurs had only been recognized as a separate species thirty years earlier, so Joseph Tyrrell was not sure what kind of creature he was looking at. However, the summer before, he had worked packing fossils. He knew that his find was important. He couldn't leave it there to be eroded away by wind and rain, possibly lost to the world forever.

But how could he collect this specimen, later to be named an *Albertosaurus*, without any of the equipment of a paleontologist?

Rolling plains
On the edge
of Dinosaur
Valley, the
prairie-
grassland soil
is as deep as
the height
of a 24-story
building. It
was deposited
over many
thousands
of years.

Excited, Joseph Tyrrell and his
assistants chipped the fossil skull
from the rock, using only their
hammers and an ax. Precious fossil
bone was smashed by the hammers
or broken off as they lowered the
skull down the cliff by rope.

Tyrrell had no way to pack the
bones properly and no crate or box
for them in his wagon, but he was
determined to save the skull.

There were no roads across
the prairie. For a week the wagon

jolted and bumped across the rough, unbroken grassland to Calgary. From there, Tyrrell shipped the skull by rail to the headquarters of the Geological Survey of Canada, in Ottawa.

Joseph Tyrrell never collected dinosaur bones again. He would be amazed to learn that the Royal Tyrrell Museum of Paleontology in Drumheller bears his name.

Tyrrell Museum
This world-famous museum of paleontology fits snugly into the landscape of the badlands.

Tyrrell's later years
After his dinosaur days, Tyrrell went back to looking for coal. He became a successful businessman and engineer.

Thomas Weston
Weston's interest in geology began as a boy when he polished rocks in his father's jewelry store.

Hoodoos
The badlands' hoodoos are columns of rock formed by erosion.

Brittle bones

It was five years before the Geological Survey of Canada sent a scientist to follow up on Tyrrell's amazing discovery. Eventually, in 1889, Thomas Weston and his assistants traveled down the Red Deer River in specially made boats, looking for dinosaur fossils.

Weston was in his late fifties. He was frightened of rattlesnakes and the river. Sometimes the boats went too fast, at other times they got stuck in the shallows. But soon he began finding dinosaur bones in the layers of rock and giant sandbanks that bordered the Red Deer.

Weston explored farther south than Tyrrell had, reaching the fantastic formations of what is now Dinosaur Provincial Park. Dinosaurs were everywhere he looked! He had found one of the most important

dinosaur sites in the world.

Like Tyrrell, Weston lacked the tools and equipment necessary to get the bones safely out of the deep valley. In his report to the Geological Survey he wrote, "Three pairs of hands carefully lifted our precious specimen—when to our surprise the thing crumbled into a thousand fragments." The dinosaur fossil he'd found was fragile and brittle with age.

Digging
Heat, dust, mosquitoes, and mud made digging in Dinosaur Valley difficult work for early paleontologists. It's still just as challenging!

In the end, lack of food forced Weston to abandon his search. But by then, he had collected a dozen cases of dinosaur bones to send back to Ottawa. Another ten years passed before a cart carrying a young paleontologist named Lawrence Lambe and a 13-foot (4 m) boat creaked over the muddy track to the western edge of Dinosaur Valley.

Lambe, who later gave his name to the duck-billed dinosaur *Lambeosaurus*, found the valley to be a treasure house of fossil bones. But, like the others before him, his problem was how to get them safely out of the badlands.

His cart couldn't handle the valley's tough terrain. He was too far from the river to use his boat. When he tried carrying bones out on a stretcher, most of them crumbled and fell apart.

By 1901 Lambe had a large collection of bone fragments, but he still didn't have a complete skull, let alone a full skeleton of a dinosaur.

Fossil hunter
Lawrence Lambe studied and named many Dinosaur Valley species. The *Lambeosaurus* was named after him in recognition of his work on dinosaurs.

Lambeosaurus
This is the largest duck-billed dinosaur discovered so far. It was about 50 feet (15 m) long.

Battle of the Bones

What's a gold rush? When gold was discovered in the Yukon and California, people rushed to the sites, hoping to get rich.

Meanwhile, in Wyoming and Montana, the discovery of huge dinosaurs was big news. As word leaked out about the amazing wealth of bones in Dinosaur Valley, the stage was set for the Great Canadian Bone Rush. Like a gold rush, it attracted colorful characters, ready to risk everything.

Barnum Brown

American paleontologist Barnum Brown sometimes did his bone hunting wearing a long fur coat. He was a dinosaur hunter with style. As a child, he had collected fossils on his father's farm. As a young man, he earned the nickname "Mr. Bones" and was famous for finding the first *Tyrannosaurus rex* in Montana. His dinosaur discoveries all went to the American Museum of Natural History in New York. The museum was eager for more.

One day, a Canadian rancher called John Wagner went to New York to see the dinosaur display. He told the staff he had bones just like theirs on his ranch back on the Red Deer River in Alberta. That was all Barnum Brown needed to hear. In 1910 he set out for a busy season of dinosaur hunting in Dinosaur Valley.

P.T. Barnum
Barnum Brown was named after this famous circus owner. P.T. Barnum claimed he had "the Greatest Show on Earth." Brown, a showman himself, boasted he had "the greatest show unearthed."

Brown's methods for digging and transporting bones were better than Weston's or Lambe's. News that he'd found a small horned dinosaur called *Leptoceratops* delighted the New York museum. "Keep quiet about this find," they advised Brown. "Get the best specimens before other explorers find them."

Soon Canadians began to realize that national treasures were being shipped out of the country. There was a public outcry, but there was no way to stop Barnum Brown.

Instead, one of the world's best-known dinosaur collectors was hired, with his sons, to collect for a new museum in Ottawa.

The four Sternbergs were called a dinosaur dream team.

Charles H. Sternberg, the father, had hunted fossils as a boy in New York State. He passed on his passion for dinosaurs to his sons, George, Charlie, and Levi. Working together, the Sternbergs created even better ways of protecting bones in burlap and plaster of Paris.

Spy?
George Sternberg started working on Barnum Brown's team. But when they accused him of spying for his father, he switched sides!

Charles Sternberg
Charles wasn't a trained paleontologist but a talented amateur. He devoted most of his life to collecting large fossils in Wyoming and Alberta.

17

Corythosaurus
This plant-eating dinosaur was one of the first found by the Sternbergs.

Important park
The Sternbergs' work helped to establish Dinosaur Provincial Park, now a UNESCO World Heritage Site.

The Sternbergs set out for Dinosaur Valley in 1912 to compete with Barnum Brown and his team of dinosaur hunters.

Over the next four years each group tried to outdo the other in making spectacular dinosaur discoveries. Sometimes, they trespassed on each other's quarries. Complaints flew back and forth, but the work went on.

Who won the Battle of the Bones? Everyone. In the four years that Barnum Brown and the Sternbergs worked in the badlands, they removed railroad cars of fossil bones. Many new species were discovered. For the next fifty years the dinosaur skeletons they collected were sorted, classified, and displayed in Ottawa,

New York, and museums around the world.

During the First World War, the Sternbergs sent specimens to the British Museum of Natural History. A ship carrying Sternberg's duck-billed dinosaur—with skin as well as bones—was torpedoed and sunk. It still lies deep in the ocean. Maybe some day, underwater paleontologists will dive for it.

Dino homes
The famous American Museum of Natural History in New York City is one of the many places that benefited from the work of bone hunters in Dinosaur Valley.

Have pick, will dig
Charles Sternberg and his family spent many years on hillsides like this one, carefully digging with hand tools to find fossils.

19

How to become a paleontologist
- Get good grades in high-school science and math.
- Visit fossil exhibits in museums.
- Study biology and geology in college.
- Volunteer on digs.

Royal Ontario Museum
The Royal Ontario Museum features a gallery with displays of dinosaurs in their habitats.

DinoStar, Philip Currie

In 1955, when Philip Currie was six, a plastic dinosaur fell out of his cereal box. He collected the whole series. At 10, Philip read a book about the work of a paleontologist. He dreamed of looking for dinosaurs when he grew up. Visiting his favorite dinosaur display at the Royal Ontario Museum in Toronto, he noticed that most of the fossils had been found in the Red Deer River Valley.

After college, Currie got a job at the Tyrrell Museum. One day, his camera case slid down a slope onto the skull of a *Daspletosaurus.* He realized he was the first living thing to see that bone in more than 75 million years. Interested in more than just collecting bones, he wanted to know how this and other dinosaurs lived, had babies, and died.

Philip Currie searched through Barnum Brown's old notes, sure that Brown had overlooked important evidence in his rush to collect and transport new finds.

Brown's 1911 notes, found in a New York museum's basement, led Currie's team to uncover a quarry on the side of a steep Dinosaur Valley cliff. It contained many *Albertosaurus* bones, plus the skeleton of a large plant-eater, a *Hypacrosaurus*.

Sacrum
The triangular bone near the base of the spine is called the sacrum.

The plant-eater's sacrum, the heaviest part of its backbone, was intact. Excited, the team wanted to get it safely to the Tyrrell Museum. A helicopter crew from a nearby British army base offered to help. The helicopter lifted the huge bundle of plaster and bone, suspended in a sling. It swung back and forth. The helicopter started to sway too, then tip dangerously. The pilot had to have the rope cut, and the precious *Hypacrosaurus* sacrum smashed into the valley floor!

Giganotosaurus
Philip Currie has traveled the globe searching for small birdlike dinosaurs and huge relatives of *Giganotosaurus*.

From dig to display

On another occasion, when Philip Currie spotted a weathered ankle bone, he thought it probably belonged to a plant-eater, the most common dinosaur in the valley. But Darren Tanke, a paleontological technician, explored further. He realized the bone belonged to a much rarer dinosaur—a tyrannosaur, a meat-eater.

Not only that, but the whole leg was there, with its bones still attached to one another. This was extremely rare. Now if they could just find the rest of the animal!

First, more foot bones were found, then ribs, hips, and the animal's right arm. It was the first time a tyrannosaur's arm had been found in one piece. At last the scientists could find out how the bones of the small arm fitted together.

Most exciting of all, the dinosaur's entire tail was preserved—all 40 vertebrae. The last tiny vertebra was only as big as an apple seed.

By this time, they realized they had found the almost complete skeleton of a young *Albertosaurus.* Now, if they could only locate her head! It turned out that Darren Tanke had been sitting on it when he first uncovered her ankle bone. The skull was buried under a layer of sandstone.

Darren Tanke
When Tanke was in high school he wrote a 600-page book on dinosaurs and sent it to Philip Currie. He was invited to go on a dig and later to join the Tyrrell Museum team as a technician.

Peaceful plant-eaters
Hadrosaurs, the plant-eaters of Dinosaur Valley, chewed on leafy vegetation such as giant ferns. Compared to carnivores, they were peaceful animals.

25

What is a coulee?
Dinosaur Valley fossil bones are sometimes found in the flat bottoms of coulees—ravines that are usually dry in summer.

Taking pictures
A photographer carefully records each discovery before fossil bones are removed. The specimen's surroundings give important clues to how the animal lived and died.

Luckily, they wouldn't need a helicopter to remove the young *Albertosaurus*. She lay in a coulee, a fairly flat area where there was room to dig and no danger of falling off a cliff.

First, the field crew dug trenches all around her bones. They separated her skeleton into five sections to make it easier to move. Then each section was covered

carefully with paper and wrapped in plaster-soaked burlap. The work took only a few weeks. Then the team was ready to move the prize skeleton to the lab. There they could study the young dinosaur and prepare her bones for display to museum visitors. She would be a prize exhibit!

But how could they get the bundle with the skull and torso out of the badlands? At almost a ton (800 kg), it would take a bulldozer just to move it! They solved the problem by renting a tractor with a huge winch to load the bundle into a dumpster and drag it to the Tyrrell Museum.

Block and tackle
A pulley system called a block and tackle is often used to hoist the heavy bones from the site.

GPS
A Global Positioning System receiver is used to pinpoint the exact location of each discovery.

It took a few weeks to dig the young *Albertosaurus* free. It took five years to prepare her for display. When lab technicians chipped away the plaster covering, they discovered that she was too fragile to risk displaying as a three-dimensional model. The slightest pressure could fracture her delicate, hollow bones.

They decided to display her inside a glass case, lying just as she was found, on her side.

When she was almost ready for display, technicians worked through the night before her opening—and one of them broke one of her ribs! The damage was repaired and, at last, a 440-pound (200 kg) sheet of glass was lowered onto the case. The team breathed a sigh of relief. Now she was protected from humidity, dust, and accidents.

In addition to becoming a major attraction at the museum, this skeleton would provide scientists with important information about the young dinosaur's environment and the way she lived and died.

Fossil drill
Technicians use tools much like dentists' drills to separate waste rock from fossils.

Hands on!
Visitors are encouraged to touch as well as look at many exhibits at the Tyrrell Museum.

Ancient secrets revealed

Philip Currie describes himself as a detective, searching for clues to a death. But, as he says, the evidence is 75 million years old, some of it has been lost, and there are no witnesses.

Despite these drawbacks, Currie and his workers used the bone record to imagine how the young female *Albertosaurus* died. She was extraordinary because almost all of her skeleton was complete, right down to the tiniest bone at the tip of her tail.

As we know, they had found her alone in an ancient riverbed in Dinosaur Provincial Park. Had she somehow become separated from her pack? Had she been too slow to keep up?

Two wounds on the right side of her body might explain the lack of speed that perhaps lead to her death. One was an injury to a toe bone, the other a broken shin. Both injuries happened before she died. The leg injury had developed a growth called a bone spur, which must have caused her great pain. Was it caused by a battle with an *Anklyosaurus* whose heavy, clubbed tail could have broken her shin bone at just that spot?

Ankylosaurus tail
This fossil of the bony club from an *Ankylosaurus*'s tail is the size of two basketballs. Imagine being walloped by that!

Learning from fossils
By examining bones, experts can learn how an animal lived and sometimes even how it died.

But death wasn't the end for the young *Albertosaurus*. She was quickly covered by sand and other sediments, which hardened into rock.

Over the years, as she lay buried deep beneath the prairie, fossilization processes took place. Organic (living) matter in her bones was replaced by minerals or inorganic materials. And the porous spaces inside her bones were filled with minerals from the water seeping through the layers of sediment.

Then, at the end of the last ice age, 10,000 years ago, an ancient glacial lake burst through its dam.

Sandstone formations
Harder layers of sedimentary rock survive erosion while layers underneath are washed away by wind and water. The result is strangely shaped formations.

The water washed down the Red Deer River Valley with such force that it carved the cliffs and some of the fantastic shapes of the badlands, right down to the layers where the *Albertosaurus* lay hidden.

Finally, after 76 million years, wind and water eroded the layers of rock covering her body, exposing the dark-brown ankle bone that Philip Currie found in 1991.

Coming out of the dirt
Scientists carve through the softer sandstone to discover the hardened fossils hidden within the layers of rock.

Why so many skeletons?

Now and then
Today the badlands are eroded and barren (above), but when dinosaurs roamed here the valley would have looked more like the landscape below.

The young *Albertosaurus* was just one of at least 500 skeletons of many different species of dinosaurs that have been found here.

Why is this valley such a great place to look for dinosaurs, despite its tough terrain, heat, and dust?

The badlands weren't always bad. 70 million years ago this was a terrific place to live—if you were a dinosaur! The fertile landscape provided the plant-eaters with plenty to eat. And the plant-eaters were food for bands of savage meat-eaters.

The area was also an ideal place to end up as a fossil. Storms and floods quickly buried dinosaurs' bodies in sand and mud, so the bones weren't scattered or destroyed.

The layers of sand and silt became rock as more layers were added. The dinosaur bones became fossils. They might have stayed deeply buried but, as we've learned, meltwater from the last ice age carved away layers of rock like a giant power hose, creating the badlands. As the rocks continue to erode, more skeletons are revealed every year.

Era/Period	Millions of Years Ago
Cenozoic Era	0–65
Mesozoic Era	65–251
Cretaceous Period	65–144
Jurassic Period	144–200
Triassic Period	200–251
Paleozoic Era	251–545
Precambrian Era	545–4.6 billion

Telling dinosaur time
Scientists divide the past into "eras" and "periods," lasting millions of years, based on the types of animals that lived in those times. Here are the main such divisions of the past. The three "periods" listed were when most of the dinosaurs lived.

Bone fossils rarely reveal information about fur or skin. Occasionally, a dinosaur was mummified, skin and all. In other cases, skin left imprints in rocks.

Dinosaur hall of fame

Albertosaurus

[al-BERT-o-SAW-rus]

This two-legged meat-eater had teeth like giant bread knives. With one snap, they could crack the bones of their prey. Like birds today, it had hollow bones and three-toed feet. Its tiny arms ended in two-fingered hands.

Of all the dinosaurs found in Dinosaur Valley, the *Albertosaurus* is probably the most famous. But for nearly 60 years after Tyrrell's discovery, it didn't have a name! In 1905, the year Alberta became a province, it was named in the province's honor.

Edmontosaurus
[ed-MON-toh-SAW-rus]

The slow-moving *Edmontosaurus* was an easy catch for the *Albertosaurus*. Its bill was toothless. The grinding teeth in its cheeks were used to munch vegetation, not fight off predators.

These plant-eaters are called "duck-billed" because of their flat faces. The fossil of a mummified *Edmontosaurus*, discovered by the Sternbergs in Wyoming in 1908, had loose skin around its nose that it could blow up like a balloon. Perhaps it made a noise when released. It had skin like knobbly leather and a bony ridge along its neck, back, and tail.

Excellent specimens of *Edmontosaurus* have been found in Dinosaur Valley.

Duck-billed dinosaurs
Some duck-billed dinosaurs like the *Edmontosaurus* were flat-headed, and some had fantastic head crests. All of them had lots of teeth—as many as two thousand—to grind up tough vegetation such as ferns, twigs, and pine needles. *Edmontosaurus* was named by Lawrence Lambe in 1917.

Big bite

The jaw of a *Gorgosaurus*, with its backward-curving teeth, was so strong that it could crush its victim's bones and swallow mouthfuls without chewing.

Gorgon

Gorgons are depicted in different ways—often with snakes for hair or with three heads—but they are always frightening and ugly like the *Gorgosaurus*.

Gorgosaurus [GOR-GO-SAW-rus]

Gorgosaurus was a carnivore, as big and ferocious as *Albertosaurus*. Its large head, curved teeth, and powerful legs made it a swift killer.

Gorgosaurus means "Gorgon lizard." It was named after the Gorgons, who were monsters in Greek mythology.

The *Gorgosaurus* was first found in Montana. Later, during the Battle of the Bones, Charlie Sternberg found a specimen of a *Gorgosaurus* in Dinosaur Valley. Lawrence Lambe named it in 1914. More than 20 specimens have now been found in Dinosaur Valley.

Styracosaurus
[sty-RACK-oh-SAW-rus]

This four-footed plant-eater was a fast runner. It charged its enemies like a rhinoceros. Its attacker would have felt the six spikes that stuck out from its head, as well as its long horn.

Bone beds in Dinosaur Valley have told paleontologists that the *Styracosaurus* traveled in herds, probably for protection. Lawrence Lambe named it in 1913.

Speed and spikes
Scientists believe the *Styracosaurus* may have reached speeds of 18 mph (30 km/h). Some specimens have head spikes longer than others. These may have been adult males.

Troodon

[TROH-oh-don]

The *Troodon* was a small carnivore, about 6 feet (2 m) long, but its size didn't stop it from being a deadly hunter. It had large eyes to hunt in low light, and long legs for speed and quick turning. Its teeth were sharp, jagged, and curved to tear into flesh. (Troodon means "wounding tooth.") But its greatest weapon was its intelligence.

The *Troodon* was one of the first dinosaurs to be discovered in Dinosaur Valley. But until Philip Currie discovered its jawbone in 1983, this dinosaur was thought to be a lizard.

Who came up with *dinosaur*? Richard Owen, a British expert on animal skeletons, coined the term *dinosaur* in 1841. The name means "terrible lizard" in Greek.

Ankylosaurus
[an-KILE-oh-SAW-rus]

How do you fight off an *Albertosaurus?* If you're an *Ankylosaurus*, you have a clublike tail and one swing of it breaks the *Albertosaurus*'s leg. Bony armor segments the size of dinner plates cover your back. With spikes around your head and along your back, you would have been a match for many meat-eaters.

Thick skulls
This skull belonged to a relative of *Ankylosaurus*, called *Euoplocephalus* [you-op-lo-SEF-ah-lus]. They both had well-protected heads, armored backs, and clubbed tails. They looked frightening but they ate only plants.

41

Animals of the late Cretaceous period included birds, frogs, turtles, fish, lizards, and small shrewlike mammals.

Fish fossil
Fossils of sea life from the Cretaceous period are well preserved. Their bones hardened to rock as the mud where they lay was slowly turned to stone.

Dinosaurs disappear

About 65 million years ago, all the dinosaurs vanished, not only from Dinosaur Valley but from everywhere on Earth. No one is sure why, but there are many theories.

The Loss of Habitat Theory

Fossil records from Dinosaur Valley and elsewhere show that many species of dinosaurs were beginning to die out before they completely disappeared. Why? Plant life may have begun to change, and the herbivores couldn't adapt. When they began to die, so did the carnivores that ate them.

The Giant Meteor Theory

A massive meteor is thought to have crashed to Earth. The explosion killed many large dinosaurs and the rest died when dust from the explosion changed the weather.

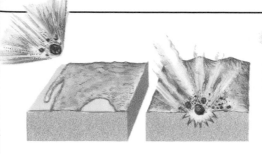

The Catastrophe Theories

These theories suggest that great upheavals on Earth caused the extinction. Increased volcanic activity may have changed the climate, killing off the dinosaurs. Perhaps the sun cooled for a period, and the dinosaurs couldn't adapt. Or a nearby star exploded, showering the earth with deadly radiation.

Craters
A giant meteor smashing into the earth left a large crater in the seabed near Mexico. It hit the earth at just about the same time as the dinosaurs mysteriously disappeared around 65 million years ago.

Come and visit
There's more to do in Dinosaur Valley than stroll through a museum. The staff at the museum and at Dinosaur Provincial Park want their visitors to get involved!

Claw
Some dinosaurs, like the *Troodon*, had a deadly claw on each of its second toes that could be swiveled upward when the animal ran.

Do and discover

Lying stretched out on the ground are two members of the Royal Tyrrell Museum's staff. They are painstakingly chipping and brushing away the soft rock. A group of young, excited faces are

watching. All around them is the harsh but beautiful terrain of the badlands.

The young observers are spending a week at the museum's Science Camp, sleeping in teepees under the stars. Today they're on a dinosaur hunt, yesterday they spent time at the museum, and tomorrow they'll canoe down the Red Deer River.

Dinosaur Valley is one of the best places in the world to look for dinosaur bones, and these young paleontologists are discovering some of the wide range of exhibits, hikes, and activities offered by the museum and Dinosaur Provincial Park.

Exhibits
Exhibits in Dinosaur Valley display the rich fossil finds from the area. Some exhibits also try to re-create the habitat in which the dinosaurs lived 65 million years ago.

Centrosaurus
Looking like an enormous rhinoceros, the *Centrosaurus* was a plant-eater with a large horn on the front of its skull and a huge frill at the back.

Fossil eggs
Hundreds of fossil eggs have been recovered from bone beds in Montana and other localities. Some contain the fossil embryos of unhatched dinosaurs.

To get up close to the badlands, visitors can camp under the hoodoos in Dinosaur Provincial Park's campground, and wake up to the sun rising over the valley.

Almost every year a new dinosaur species is discovered in the park. Hiking there takes you close to the work of real paleontologists. Activities vary, but you might be able to join the Fossil Safari Hike, a guided walk to a working fossil site. A short hike on the Trail of the Fossil Hunters takes you to the fossil sites that Barnum Brown discovered. And the Centrosaurus Bone Bed Hike leads to an area the size of two tennis courts that was a world-famous fossil site in the 1980s. This is where paleontologists

discovered the fossils of a herd of dinosaurs who died at the same time.

Every day in Dinosaur Valley, something exciting can happen. No wonder nearly half a million people visit the museum and the surrounding badlands each year. Maybe if you go to the valley, you'll come across a fossil, too. Who knows? You might grow up to be a dinosaur hunter like Philip Currie!

Tours of the park
A tour guide explains the route to visitors. Remember the rules—if you find a fossil, don't disturb it! Alert a member of the team.

Glossary

Badlands
A region of dry barren land marked by gullies, hoodoos, and other unusual rock formations caused by erosion. The name "badlands" came from the belief that these lands were of little use.

Carnivore
A meat-eating animal.

Cretaceous period
A period of time from 65–144 million years ago. Dinosaurs became extinct at the end of this period.

Dig
An expedition to remove fossils or human artifacts from layers of rock.

Erosion
The gradual wearing away and movement of rock or soil caused by water, wind, or ice.

Fossil
The remains of living things preserved in rock. Some fossils are skeletons, others are impressions of skin or footprints.

Geology
The science of the earth's crust—its layers, composition, and history.

Glacial
Relating to the effects of glaciers or an ice age.

Habitat
The environment that an animal or plant usually lives in.

Hoodoo
A pillar or column of rock created by rapid erosion.

Mammal
A type of animal that is warm-blooded, is covered in hair, and gives birth to live young which it nourishes with milk.

Meltwater
Water from melting glaciers or snow.

Meteor
A mass of stone or metal that hurtles from outer space toward Earth with enormous speed and heat.

Paleontology
The study of fossil remains of plants and animals. The name comes from the Greek word *palaios,* meaning ancient.

Plaster jacket
A covering made of hardened plaster and burlap used to wrap fossils for protection.

Predators
Animals that kill and eat other living animals.

Quarry
In paleontology, a site where fossils are found and removed from the ground.

Sandstone
Rock made of grains of sand cemented together.

Sedimentary rock
Rock made of layers of sediment—material that has been deposited by wind or water. Sandstone is a sedimentary rock.

Species
A group of living things that can breed in the wild and are different only in small details.

Specimen
A plant or animal used as an example of its species for study or display.

Tyrannosaur
A member of a family of large, meat-eating dinosaurs. *T. rex* and *Albertosaurus* are examples.

UNESCO World Heritage Site
A natural world heritage site is a region designated by the United Nations for special protection because of its outstanding beauty and/or scientific importance.

Vertebrae
A series of small bones forming the backbone of an animal.